Passing
through the
Woods

Selected Poems by

David Gwilym Anthony

Foreword by
Catherine Chandler

Cover illustration by
Merfyn C Davies

Copyright © David Gwilym Anthony 2012

The moral right of the author has been asserted.

Apart from any fair dealing for the purposes of research or private study, or criticism or review, as permitted under the Copyright, Designs and Patents Act 1988, this publication may only be reproduced, stored or transmitted, in any form or by any means, with the prior permission in writing of the publishers, or in the case of reprographic reproduction in accordance with the terms of licences issued by the Copyright Licensing Agency. Enquiries concerning reproduction outside those terms should be sent to the publishers.

Matador
9 Priory Business Park
Kibworth Beauchamp
Leicestershire LE8 0RX, UK
Tel: (+44) 116 279 2299
Fax: (+44) 116 279 2277
Email: books@troubador.co.uk
Web: www.troubador.co.uk/matador

ISBN 978 1780882 741

British Library Cataloguing in Publication Data.
A catalogue record for this book is available from the British Library.

Typeset in Garamond by Troubador Publishing Ltd

Matador is an imprint of Troubador Publishing Ltd

Printed in Great Britain by the MPG Books Group, Bodmin and King's Lynn

Foreword

By Catherine Chandler, Author of *Lines of Flight*

Passing through the Woods comprises a superb collection of Welsh poet David Gwilym Anthony's most memorable poems from his previous books, *Words to Say* and *Talking to Lord Newborough*, as well as a selection of excellent new pieces.

In *Passing through the Woods*, David regales the reader with a variety of skillfully crafted, sensitively rendered poems in both formal and free verse, whose tone and subject matter range from the playful (the witty quip "Walking the Dog"), to the philosophical (the roundel "Flotsam on a Winter's Tide"), to the utterly and immediately painful (the triolet "Mother's Day").

David's greatest strength, however, lies in his exquisite sonnets, and the reader is treated to well over two dozen of them, in various permutations, in *Passing through the Woods*. Especially beautiful are "Bloodlines", "Flower Seller", "One-Way Ticket", "Water Bearer", "Crossing the Border" and "Remembered Wings". My favourite is the stately and powerful "Wede Away", the sonnet David submitted to the Eratosphere Sonnet Bake-off which I hosted in 2009 in conjunction with the late Turner Cassity, a sonnet British poet Alan Wickes termed a 'timeless classic' that 'stands up well amongst famous antecedents' such as John McCrae's "In Flanders Fields" and "Les lilas et les roses" by Louis Aragon.

"Wede Away" means "withered away" in Scots dialect. It is a reference to "The Flowers of the Forest", a lament the Scots often play at the funerals of those who died early. Played on the bagpipes, it is the official lament of the Canadian Army, a tune only too frequently played in recent years since Operation Enduring Freedom began. Being a Canadian by choice, as well as a proud American by birth, and the cousin of a young man killed in Vietnam, I read this poem ('pale soldier roses, rearguard in retreat') as one might expect, as a sorrowful funeral dirge but also as a powerful anti-war hymn, where flags and flowers are poor comfort for those who live on.

I found that each of the flowers that are named in the poem has been assigned contradictory symbolism, depending on the source, both positive and negative, and I believe they were chosen with great care. For example, wisteria (also the first word in the poem) is a symbol both of youth and longevity as well as of memory and honor. Hyacinths are known as emblems of sports and youth, but also refer to sorrow and resignation. Poppies can mean wealth, pleasure and success, as well as eternal sleep, rest, and death. The honeysuckle, though, has one meaning only: devoted fraternal affection and love.

But it is the soldier rose that had me perplexed. As Mr. Cassity pointed out, roses are not usual military symbols. And my symbolism dictionary contains dozens of types of roses, but no reference to the soldier rose. Finally, Wikipedia came through, with a description of the *hibiscus militaris*, also known as the soldier rose. The article states, 'These flowers require exposure to sunlight to open up properly, and then last only a single day.' Then, the plant reseeds itself and, though its stalk dies down in the winter, it grows back in the spring. This is the most significant flower of all those named in the poem. "Wede Away"

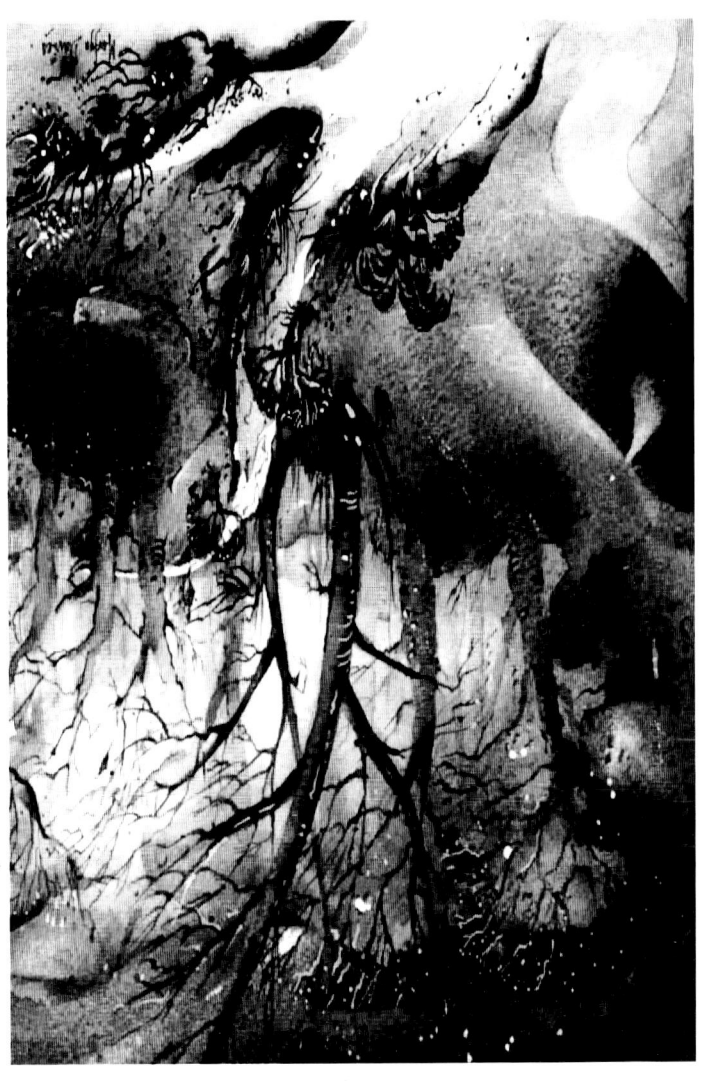

cannot leave the reader, of any age, indifferent. I chose this sonnet because it is true to the spirit of the sonnet in so many ways, not least of which is how it takes a very personal experience and transforms it into what Rossetti called 'a moment's monument, – /Memorial from the Soul's eternity/To one dead deathless hour'.

Whether the poems in *Passing through the Woods* happen to deal with ostensibly familiar themes such as the weather ("Warming" in hymnal stanza), death and destruction (the villanelle "Plague"), the writing life (the sonnet "Bird's Eye View"), or exotic landscapes (the tanka "Four Views of Kyoto"), David Anthony's keen eye and empathic response to the people, places and things he observes provide an intersection of the universal and the particular that cannot fail to resonate with readers throughout the English-speaking world. They are poems without borders.

Finally, as the prepositional phrase in the book's title intimates, we are all merely 'passing through'. And although we are not out of the woods just yet, and though along the way our hearts will be broken by 'the little things' ("Words to Say") as well as by the big ones, David Anthony's honest, compassionate poems in *Passing through the Woods* are the perfect companions for the journey.

CONTENTS

Journeys	**1**
Passing through the Woods	2
Summer's End	3
Flotsam on a Winter's Tide	4
Father of the Man	5
The Road Taken	6
Walking the Dog	7
In a Storm	8
Gatekeepers	9
Navigator	10
Partings	**11**
A Winter Funeral	12
Unsaid	13
I Thought You Were a Friend	14
Remembered Wings	15
Who'll Hold Their Hands?	16
Out of the Night	17
Nearer to Thee	18
Words to Say	19
To Die For	20
On the Death of the Queen Mother	21
Mother's Day	22
On the Suicide of a Friend	23
A La Cart	24

Seasons	**25**
Wede Away	26
Hawthorn	27
Tallyman	28
Late August at Hadrian's Wall	29
English Weathercock	30
Older the Worse	31
Warming	32
In Search of Inspiration	**33**
Triolet	34
Stuffing it In	35
My Bulkhead Light	36
Slush Pile	37
To My Muse	38
On first looking into Chapman's Homer	39
Bird's Eye View	40
Perspectives	**41**
For All the Saints	42
Knowing the Score	43
Crossing the Border	44
Plague	45
Water Bearer	46
Talking to Lord Newborough	47
To Gerard Manley Hopkins	48

People and Places — 49

- One-Way Ticket — 50
- Situation Vacant — 51
- Saint Patrick's Day Parade, Yokohama — 52
- Four Views of Kyoto — 53
- Tambourine Man — 54
- Heilige Nacht — 55
- Over America — 56
- Look Away — 57
- Pickett's Charge — 58
- Flower Seller — 59
- Who's Afraid? — 60
- Bloodlines — 61
- On a Photograph of a Young Child — 62
- For My Daughter — 63
- Harry Potter — 64
- Cushioning the Blow — 65

- About the author — 66
- Poets' comments on David's books — 67
- And on his poems — 71
- Index of Poems — 73

ACKNOWLEDGEMENTS

I had intended to produce a second edition of my book *Talking to Lord Newborough*, published by Jaimes Alsop's Alsop Review Press. Sadly Jaimes died and the press is no longer in existence. *Passing through the Woods* contains many of the poems in *Talking to Lord Newborough* with revisions, along with new poems. Some of these poems have appeared in the following books and magazines:

UK
Acumen, Candelabrum, Hand Luggage Only (Shortlist Anthology of Open Poetry's 2007 International Sonnet Competition), *The London Magazine, Poetry Scotland, Snakeskin, The Sonnet at the Millennium* (Anthology*), The Sun Also Rises, Unsuitable Companions* (Chapbook), *Worm, Write-away*

USA & Internet
Angle, Anthology One (Alsop Review Press), *Artemis Journal, Avatar Review, The Barefoot Muse, The Buckeye, Bumbershoot, Carnelian, Defenestration, Edge City Review, The Eleventh Muse, First Things, The Flea, 14 by 14, Here and Now, The HyperTexts, Lighten Up Online, Light Quarterly, Lilt, Mindfire Renewed, The New Formalist, Octavo, Pierian Springs, Poems for Big Kids* (Anthology), *Shit Creek Review, Soundzine, The Susquehanna Quarterly, Umbrella, Writer's Hood*

JAPAN
Contemporary Ten Thousand Leaves Anthology (Gendai Manyo Shu), Eisuke Shiiki's *Ran Pan Un, Tanka Journal*

Journeys

Passing through the Woods

It's hard to see my way because
the leaves have fallen. Now
they're drifting where a path once was —
it's hard to see my way. Because
the light is brief I dare not pause;
I'll find the track somehow.
It's hard to see my way because
the leaves have fallen now.

Summer's End

Yesterday,
stealing from the sun,
dandelions
lit the shaded path
briefly. Now they're gone.

Hurry through
faded meadows, while
light still holds.
Days grow shorter; how
quickly evening comes.

Stirred to rise
by a falling foot,
feathered seeds,
graceful on the breeze,
drift towards the dawn.

Flotsam on a Winter's Tide

Round again on the full tide, churning
close to the quiet foreshore, then
caught by the undertow and turning
round again —

slowing now: as far-travelled men,
turning back with regret or yearning,
pause for a while near a journey's end.

Knowing all and beyond all knowing,
Nature speaks in the tide's turn when
all that drifts is gathered going
round again.

Father of the Man

While wandering the wastelands of my mind,
uncertain where the hazy pathways led
and frightened by the darkness up ahead,
I saw my Youth approaching from behind
and paused and waited, thinking what to say.
We'd broken contact many years ago —
we hadn't much in common. Even so
his certainty might help me find the way.

He came to meet me coldly with a frown,
and I fell silent, angered, filled with such
resentment that this parent asked so much,
mixed with regret because I'd let him down.

So burdened by the weight of wasted days
I left him and we went our separate ways.

The Road Taken

Youth's urgency permitted no delay
and many paths diverged. I didn't know
which one to take or where I ought to go,
and settled for a broad and trodden way
because it offered light and company;
but as my friends dispersed along the road
I travelled on alone and often strode
in haste through where I had no wish to be.

At evening everything becomes opaque,
and circumstance has turned the track I chose
back on itself, much nearer now to those
remembered byways I shall never take.
This is a light to me when dark is near:
the paths diverged but all at last led here.

Walking the Dog

My aged Lab had ambled on ahead
to greet a passer-by, who paused to pet her.

"A little old, a little lame," she said.
"You're right," said I, "nor is my dog much better."

In a Storm

With my shaggy old dog I decided to go
through the mountains to see Uncle Jim.
We'd walked a few miles when it started to snow,
and conditions were soon looking grim.

Those hills are not friendly when bitter winds blow
and your torch is beginning to fail.
We were cheered by the sight of a light far below,
and we fought our way there through the gale.

It was Pedro's — a Portuguese bar you may know:
it's famous for fortified wine.
Said Pedro, "Sit down by the fire's warming glow;
once you've had a few drinks you'll be fine.

"I have ruby and white and I've tawny also
from Sandeman, Taylor and Dow —
fine vintages all. I don't keep them for show;
take your pick and I'll pour it right now."

I called for a glass of each vintage, although
I ought to drink tea to get warm,
having sworn to steer clear of the booze. Even so,
I will try any port in a storm.

Gatekeepers

His spaniel rushed to greet him when he died.
A splendid golden gate marked Heaven was near.
A Seraph said, "Dogs aren't allowed in here,
but you, my friend, are welcome; step inside."
He thought a moment, turned and walked away.
They found a gate, marked Heaven once again,
where angels looked like ordinary men
and showed them where a graceful city lay,
explaining that the other place was Hell.
"Aren't you concerned," he asked, "when they proclaim
such falsehoods, misappropriate your name,
and try to steal your people's souls as well?"
"No, not at all; no cause for us to mind:
they take the folk who'd leave their friends behind."

Navigator

I raised the anchor; sails flashed out unfurled,
then filled; I set a course, *h t t p://*—
and started out across a cyber sea
in search of fellow feeling in the world.
I wandered where the winter seas were pearled
with scattered islands of affinity,
whose harbours sometimes seemed like home to me,
calm havens when distress and discord swirled.

Seafarers slightly known and swiftly gone,
some here to listen, some with things to say:
those strangers warming in the light that shone
from empathy had little time to stay.
Minds met a moment, touched and travelled on
to look for something lost and far away.

Partings

A Winter Funeral

The church was cold in a sullen light
as we said goodbye to Ron.
Over the bier a moth took flight,
though the church was cold. In the sullen light
it fluttered down as a blessing might,
then gained the porch and was gone.
And the church was gold in a sudden light
as we said goodbye to Ron.

Unsaid

Cheerily… charily,
friend of my childhood, I
thought of you often yet
left things unsaid.

Lately I looked for you
seeking atonement, and
needing to talk, but I
learned you were dead.

I Thought You Were a Friend
(for MJM)

I knew you well and thought you were a friend,
and yet you gave no sign you meant to go.
Is this the proper way for it to end?

The hardest thing for me to comprehend
is why you failed to say goodbye, although
I knew you well and thought you were a friend,

and never doubted once I could depend
on you. To my regret it was not so.
Is this the proper way — for it to end

so arbitrarily? I meant to spend
more time with you. It was a cruel blow
from one I knew, and thought of as a friend.

I would have stood beside you to defend
against the fear, though all I really know
is this: the proper way for it to end

is not the way the passing-bells pretend;
they ring with falsehood, sonorous and slow.
Is this the proper way for it to end
for you who left, although you were my friend?

Remembered Wings

Year after year their timing was the same.
As early summer took the place of spring
my swallows came, and briskly gathering
would breed then raise their young and so proclaim
hope's renaissance. They darted sharp as flame
between the earth and sky, remembering
old haunts despite long miles of wandering.
This year I waited but they never came.

Autumn's a time for leaving: cherished things
are embers, as remembered flames burn low,
and vanish with the chill the first frost brings;
a time to grieve, though now it isn't so:
never to greet those brave arriving wings
spares the pain of parting when they go.

Who'll Hold Their Hands?

Sometimes an image strikes just like a blow:
I've seen deceit, behind a mask of care,
cut with a lash and flay the senses bare.
A bitter man's betraying kiss was so;
or those two children caught on video —
ignored by passers-by (not their affair) —
who took a toddler's hand and led him where
there are dark truths we do not choose to know.

"Hanging's too good!" "They don't deserve to live!"
(But whose is the betrayal we recall?)
Did Christ, the friend to thief and fugitive,
greet Judas' kiss with empathy or gall?
They were our sins and so we can't forgive:
just ten years old. May God forgive us all.

(Jamie Bulger, aged two, was abducted and killed in Bootle, Merseyside in 1993 by ten-year-olds Jon Venables and Robert Thompson.)

Out of the Night

We saw your death — they showed it on TV —
and had revenge if vengeance was our goal.
You thanked the gods, whatever gods may be,
and spoke of your unconquerable soul.
We shared a god — no, not the one whose whole
existence was compassionate, who tried
by promising redemption to console
his wayward children, and was crucified.
We chose your sterner god to be our guide,
with ancient tribal precepts and a sword.
Though Hope and Charity did not abide,
Faith lived when our uncompromising Lord —
not often merciful but always just —
demanded eye for eye and dust for dust.

(Timothy McVeigh, called the Oklahoma Bomber, who chose Henley's "Invictus" as his epitaph.)

Nearer to Thee
(in memory of Holly Wells and Jessica Chapman)

We scoured the headlines for the news
and sensed what was to come:
those children in the photograph
were not returning home.
Small hope surrendered with a bleak
announcement on TV,
and someone played a brave old tune —
Nearer, my God, to Thee.

Can God be near when malice lurks
throughout the world He made,
when every generation sees
its innocents betrayed?
Each evil lessens all of us —
Who lets such evil be?
But grief fills churches, grief and shame,
and brings us nearer Thee.

We search for meaning, finding none,
for hope where hope has died.
I think about a message sent
when Christ was crucified:
untainted lives are beacons, bright
however dark the sea.
Take them, Father; take our hopes
and hold them near to Thee.

Words to Say

The priest knew all the proper words to say.
He'd never met her but he had a note.
He mentioned everything her brother wrote
and said she'd had a good life anyway.

The old piano she would often play
still holds remembered cadences of those
Welsh melodies she loved, but I suppose
we'll sell it now that Betty's passed away.

I saw her schedules written on a chart
pinned to the study wall: she'd meant to speak
to Mum and booked the dentist for next week.
Strange, how the little things can break your heart.

I'd watched her as she faded day by day,
but never found the proper words to say.

To Die For

Aunt Bessie has a talent: when she bakes
the flavour drives you wild. My cousins say
their father, Tim, a regular gourmet,
married her for love — of chocolate cakes.

Poor Uncle Tim was feeling far from well —
in fact, was on his deathbed — when the scent
of baking half-revived him. Off he went
to find the source of that seductive smell.

Each step was painful as he tottered down
to taste the treat. At last his feeble hand
grasped hungrily. Bess slapped it sharply and
dismissed him with an irritated frown:

"Clear off to bed and put the buns back too!
I made them for the funeral, not for you."

On the Death of the Queen Mother

The sun that bravely shone at last went down.
Lie easy now, the head that wore a crown.

*(Elizabeth the Queen Mother, last Empress of India,
August 1900 — March 2002.)*

Mother's Day

I hold the phone remembering —
no need to call today.
Routine's my life raft; as I cling
I hold the phone, remembering
a loss. It is a cruel thing,
this trick the mind can play.
I hold the phone, remembering.
No need to call today.

On the Suicide of a Friend

God help the kids! I heard the neighbours say —
so quick to judge, though mostly they were kind.
They saw the sorry mess you left behind
and thought you took the coward's selfish way.

The coward's way? No, not that I can see:
despair's a snare. They say a fox will gnaw
its fettered limb and sacrifice the paw:
what desperation drove you to break free?

Nor were you selfish. Just beneath the calm
the darkness gathered; I have known it too.
It touched the ones you loved: I'm certain you
believed you were protecting them from harm.

God — if there's a God — will grant you rest:
you failed, we all do, but you did your best.

A La Cart

She heard the sound of banging at the door.
"Are you the Widow Murphy?" Jimmy cried.
"They call me Mrs Murphy, that's for sure,
but no, I ain't no widow," she replied.
Says Jim, "It may have been a fact before,
but take a look what's on me cart outside."

Seasons

Wede Away
(for JMA)

Wisteria soft against a deeper blue,
and hyacinth, youth's talisman: those bright
creations filled my wakening world with light.
I miss the flowers of spring and all things new.

Fulfilment followed promise to a time
rich with the scents and ripeness spring foretold —
honeysuckle, poppy, marigold.
I miss the flowers of summer in its prime.

Sparse as the season fades towards December,
pale soldier roses, rearguard in retreat,
still blossom as they face an old defeat,
while asters linger late into November
to hurl their small defiance at the fall.
— I'll miss the flowers of autumn most of all.

Hawthorn

Why are you weeping, May Tree, May Tree,
why are you weeping, May?
Springtime's fresh and the sun is high,
there is no blue like the morning sky
and winter's far away.
The season's glad so why be sad?
Why are you weeping, May?

Why are you weeping, May Tree, May Tree,
why are you weeping, May —
shedding tears of perfect white,
pure as sorrow and white as light,
in garlanded decay?

Is it care for seasons yet to be?
Let's look away and refuse to see:
the year's young and so are we
and winter's far away.
Thoughts so cold never trouble me,
so cease your weeping, May.

Please cease your weeping, May.

Tallyman

It seems no time since warmth replaced the cold,
and nature's careful plans were first displayed
in buds along the foxglove's stem, arrayed
profusely and preparing to unfold.

Tall tallyman, I know the price you pay:
your clustered blossoms nodding to the dawn
fade one for every evening as you mourn
the counted fall of every summer's day.

Too soon a wilder wind arriving scours
the season's bright creations, stripping bare
the hedgerows and the woodland clearings where
you sacrifice your last and lonely flowers —

still beautiful, although the best are past,
and missed the most because they were the last.

Late August at Hadrian's Wall

April's spring
and October's fall:
both so loved —
one for promises,
one for memories.

Who could love
summer's sultry close?
Changes loom:
clouds high-building drift
nearer through the haze.

August though
bears a Caesar's name,
and the year
stoic in decline
stands and holds a while.

English Weathercock

Perched proudly on the chimney stack,
my brand-new weather vane
observes the ever-changing winds
to see if it will rain.

At first the cockerel faced the West
his expectation plain.
The clouds rolled in on cue and we
had bucketloads of rain.

He next rotated North then East,
averring once again
there would be gales (and so it proved)
along with heavy rain.

Today he's veered towards the South
and points to sun-drenched Spain.
I'll take my mac and brolly then:
it's bound to pour with rain.

Older the Worse

The swing of the seasons brings small cheer:
the world grows tired and groans,
and colours once so crisp and clear
are faded monochromes.
I fear the night and I fear the light
as seed falls sterile on stones
and spring struggles harder every year
to cover winter's bones.

Warming

The seasons' course seems strange to me,
more strange than I remember.
Wild flowers bloom unseasonably:
primroses in November.

The young pretend to blame us all.
Well, youth's a great dissembler:
May was forever, I recall,
and there was no November.

These days I'll take what Nature sends
to hoard for dour December:
a glow of warmth as autumn ends;
primroses in November.

In Search of Inspiration

Triolet

I think I'll write a triolet —
but does it rhyme with get or gay?
I'm ignorant I know, and yet
I think I'll write a triolet,
and make a rhyme with gay, or get —
who gives a toss whichever way?
I think I'll write a triolet —
but does it rhyme with get or gay?

Stuffing it In

Today I feel the urge to do a sonnet:
I'll see to it before the morning's out.
Just one word rhymes with sonnet, but no doubt
a slant can be insinuated — Done it!
So far so good. Enjambment helps: let's run it
between the lines. I'm half-inclined to flout
the rule insisting on a turn, about
line nine. Screw Petrarch's horse! Who'd ride in on it?
But like the nag I'm knackered, so let's try
to reach a lazy climax; soon be there:
just ease it in, far better not to force it.
Sonnets are like those garments ladies buy —
I'm thinking of restraining underwear.
Sometimes the bulges overcome the corset.

My Bulkhead Light

My bulkhead light was broken;
I broke it yesterday.
I never meant to break it;
Alas alackaday!

It served me well and truly;
It made the darkness bright.
'Twas hammer-blow that laid it low
And robbed me of my light.

I hied me down to Do It All
And hailed the Overseer:
"Where will I find a bulkhead light?"
"We keep them over here."

My bulkhead light is mended;
I mended it today.
'Twill never be the same, though;
Alas alackaday!

Come all ye Home Improvements men,
Take heed and learn from me:
A bulkhead light costs seven pounds,
Including VAT.

Slush Pile

In some respects I like this, even though
the workmanship's not great. Who'd rhyme 'today'
with 'day'? This one's arcane: what does it *say*?
Two down now; just two hundred more to go.
Call that a poem? Prose! And this one's so
Poetic. Why must people disobey
the basic rules of syntax? No. No way,
and No, and No, and No, and No, and No,

and… Oh. Here's something special: see it shine.
It coruscates: a lamp of burnished gold
revealing vistas hitherto unseen.
I sense the presence of a noble soul
who dares to go where others have not been…
Ah, I recall it now: it's one of mine!

To My Muse

Unpin your long tresses and let them unfurl;
unfasten your brassiere too.
Then put on these tassels and give them a twirl:
I'm planning to… contemplate you.

I see your attention is drawn to my jeans:
my pocket conceals a big pen.
I'll whip it out gladly. You know what it means:
I'm happy to see you again.

I tend to forget what goes where, when and how:
it's been a long time, you can tell.
But it's all flooding back in a torrent right now,
so take off your knickers as well.

On first looking into Chapman's Homer
(with apologies to John Keats)

I'd never read Chapman before
and felt like that sky-watcher (Moore);
or those blokes on a peak
who weren't able to speak,
being gobsmacked by all that they saw.

(Prompted by a debate on the need for brevity in poetry.)

Bird's Eye View

As if I work for him — how could he know
the weight of all my cares? — a robin hops
towards me from the border; then he stops
to watch me push my mower to and fro.
He looks for worms along the fresh-cut line,
while I seek inspiration for a gem
to stun my critics — how I'll dazzle them!
The bird has his agenda; I have mine.

My chore complete, I settle down to wring
some essence from our interaction. Now
a sharp deflating insight has unfurled
its wings. (I *had* been contemplating how
absurd it was for such a little thing
to think himself the centre of the world.)

Perspectives

For All the Saints

For you, brave martyr-saints whose blood
refreshed the faith my fathers knew;
and you, ascetic hermit-saints
who lived where lonely wormwood grew;
and you, remorseless soldier-saints
who spread the Word with swords, and slew
wild unrepentant heathen hordes
in Jesus' name: I pray for you.
I pray your unrelenting cause
is not unworthy, or untrue.

Knowing the Score

The slights I cherish sing to me
their old seductive song:
it's friends who always wound the worst —
the list I keep is long.
I don't much like the counterpoint,
a quiet voice but strong:
"Choose wisely when remembering;
love keeps no count of wrong."

(1 Corinthians 13)

Crossing the Border

Fences are never needed: Herdwick sheep,
waking the Lakeland hills with wistful bleating,
have learned the boundaries they are to keep.
Fierce Viking settlers recognised the greeting
of each flock heafted to its native fell,
and cared for them through hardship, knowing well
how troubles pass and all revives with spring.
Now come the slaughter men, their guns depleting
ancient herds, and old ways are retreating:
can thought deny the soul's remembering?
May we return some part of all we take,
and so reclaim the wisdom, lost to man,
to know our bounds; then nature shall remake
a truer borderline than fences can.

(Herdwicks: specific to the hills of Cumbria, near the England/Scotland border, with a homing instinct, known as "heafting" in Cumbrian dialect, which was nearly destroyed by mass slaughter during the foot and mouth epidemic.)

Plague

The guns are loud across the land tonight.
Grim beacon flames flash out from shire to shire
and horror groans without an end in sight.

Best not to look as marksmen expedite
such slaughter. Hired to empty every byre,
the guns are loud. Across the land tonight

spring flinches at the foulness of the blight
that lurks within the pall above each pyre,
and horror groans without an end, in sight

of pallid flames where all is darkly bright.
So draw the blinds and turn the music higher —
the guns are loud across the land tonight.

Send off the children. Let them still delight
in childish things; don't tell them life's a liar
and horror groans. Without an end in sight

there seems no point. Why carry on, why fight?
Not only cattle perish in the fire,
and horror groans without an end in sight.
The guns are loud across the land tonight.

*(English foot and mouth epidemic, spring 2001,
when seven million animals were slaughtered.)*

Water Bearer

Each dawn, before the sun devoured the shade
and seared the arid land, a potter strode
down to the well along a dusty road
to fill a well-used water jar he'd made.

As he returned one day a stranger said,
"Your jar is fractured. Anyone can see
you waste your time and labour fruitlessly.
The water spills along the track you tread."

The potter answered, "Though it leaks it still
retains enough for me, and I would not,
for all its flaws, discard my battered pot.
It has a further purpose to fulfil."

Where he had passed, a radiant display
of flowers bobbed to greet the breaking day.

Talking to Lord Newborough

I'd perch beside your gravestone years ago,
a boy who thought you old at forty-three.
I knew you loved this quiet place, like me.
We'd gaze towards Maentwrog far below,
kindred spirits, and I'd talk to you.
Sometimes I asked what it was like to die —
were you afraid? You never did reply,
but silence rested lightly on us two.

These days the past is nearer, so I came
to our remembered refuge on the hill,
expecting change yet finding little there:
my village and the Moelwyns look the same,
Saint Michael's Church commands the valley still —
but you, old friend, are younger than you were.

(Lt. William Charles Wynn, 1873 — 1916, 4th Baron Newborough, whose grave overlooks the Vale of Ffestiniog in North Wales.)

To Gerard Manley Hopkins

Your spirit hovered quivering, poised on air
of sense and sound, charged like a lightning rod:
now flashing out to seize the grace of God,
now plummeting in darkness and despair —
despair! Did wisdom really bring you there,
where tired generations trod and trod,
where feet convey no feeling, being shod,
where hopelessness hangs heavy everywhere?

Sometimes I wonder, did you understand
without the dark your candle could not glow?
Your soul was tortured by self-reprimand,
self-crucified, self-loathing; yet I know
the God you loved and hated took your hand
and led you safe at last where no storms blow.

People and Places

One-Way Ticket

They closed the line and just the track remains.
The miners' railway where we used to play
in far-off summers, when I came to stay,
echoes with the ghosts of long-gone trains.

Cwm Cynfal and the Ceunant ring with wild
unchanging songs of childhood. Years away
mean nothing there. When I returned today
they called to me, and knew me as their child.

The rest is altered irretrievably.
My kin died years ago or else moved on:
no point in staying once the work was gone.
How few there are who still remember me.

My ties are broken far beyond repair:
the line is closed and just the tracks are there.

(Cwm Cynfal and the Ceunant: the valley and gorge of the River Cynfal.)

Situation Vacant

My cousins have a strong religious streak —
teetotal Bible Belters. I don't like
those Jesus freaks: the worst one's Pastor Mike.
To my surprise I heard from him last week.

He wrote, "You've met my helper Pete, I think:
I used to take him with me when I went
to spread the Word. The man was heaven-sent
to demonstrate the ill effects of drink.

He'd drool beside me in the Gospel Hall
and wet himself, then fall about the stage;
or, turning to my flock in drunken rage,
he'd stagger forth and vilify them all.

He's passed away, the poor pathetic slob;
so how about it: would you like the job?"

Saint Patrick's Day Parade, Yokohama

I went to Yokohama for Saint Patrick's Day just gone —
as rare a sight as any I have seen.
O'Sakaguchi led the way: he'd brought his big baton
and he twirled along a-wearing of the green.

Behind him came the Kamakura Firemen's Marching Band.
They played 'I'll Take You Home Again, Kathleen'.
It wasn't great for marching but we tried and, hand in hand,
we swayed along a-wearing of the green.

Next came the Kawasaki Irish Dancers: they were good,
each one a dark-eyed Japanese colleen.
Mac Nakamura piped them on to 'Maggie in the Wood'
and they jigged along a-wearing of the green.

The Tokyo Irish Setters Club had travelled down in force.
The dogs were pretty frisky, and were keen
to join the fun. In natty caps, and smartly groomed of course,
they pranced along a-wearing of the green.

They took me for an Irishman on Patrick's Day just gone
(though I'm about as Irish as the Queen),
and rushed to take my picture, since I was the only one,
as I marched along a-wearing of the green.

Four Views of Kyoto

Gion bar —
homely, far from home.
We discuss
how to change the world
and the price of beer.

Wooden shrines
ruined, rebuilt, unchanged:
how they bend
to the blows of time —
fragile permanence.

Geisha twins —
young or old, who knows?
Painted masks
safely cover old
passions, or young dreams.

Vestiges
of each age remain,
layered and
softly fading. Plum
blossom drifts on snow.

Tambourine Man
(for Bob Dylan's 60th birthday)

His hair a thicket, voice a rasping saw
cutting through cant and conscience's decay —
my scruffy hero channelled youth's dismay
and changed the world in 1964.
His music called to me: I heard with awe
wild songs — they wheeled and soared above the day
then swooping drove indifference away.
Glad to be young I stood at heaven's door.

He calls again, and how can I resist
a ragged clown behind a reverie
still chasing wraiths within the day's grey mist?
It's darker now: I cannot sense or see
a way ahead but I can dance. Hey! Mist-
-er Tambourine Man, play a song for me.

Heilige Nacht

A broken tank stands sentinel before
the salient where Rundstedt's soldiers tried
to force a passage as their army died
that bitter Christmas, 1944.
By then they knew they couldn't win the war
but fought to thrust their enemy aside —
for comrades, or obedience, or pride —
and, failing, knew they could have done no more.

Did the Child, who all those years ago
was born in hope, now look on in despair?
Perhaps, though I believe it was not so.
My thoughts return to lonely valleys where
the human spirit suffered in the snow
but still endured. It stood unbroken there.

(The German Ardennes offensive ("The Battle of the Bulge"), December 1944 – January 1945, was fought in severe cold and heavy snowfall and was halted by American counter-attacks and fuel shortages. A German tank still stands beside the road at Celles, marking the furthest point of the advance on Christmas Eve, 1944.)

Over America
*(Jeremy Glick, United Airlines
Flight 93, 11 Sept. 2001)*

A man spoke out from a lonely place
on his pocket telephone.
As he heard what end he would have to face
a man spoke out from a lonely place.
To bow to force could be no disgrace
yet he vowed to fight for his own.
A man spoke out for the human race
on his pocket telephone.

Look Away
Chancellorsville, 2 May, 1863

God-fearing Patriarch, you rose to smite
the North as Samson smote the Philistine:
the South's defender, certain of divine
endorsement, confident our cause was right.
You whipped the Yankees squarely every fight
and championed your people's proud design,
till random bullets from our picket line
killed you and so foreshadowed Dixie's night.

Come tired soldier, let us cross the stream
and rest beneath the shadow of a tree.
The centre fails; intruders reign supreme
and raze the land through Georgia to the sea.
The shadow deepens darkening a dream
as Dixie toils towards her Calvary.

("Let us cross over the river and rest under the shade of the trees" were the last words of General 'Stonewall' Jackson, shot by his own pickets.)

Pickett's Charge
Gettysburg, 3 July, 1863

Perhaps we should have waited for the night:
those Yankee guns were fierce by day. Instead,
we could have nailed them in the fading light.

The South's high-water mark lay straight ahead;
but food was short, our army badly shod,
the ammunition low and Stonewall dead.

Longstreet couldn't speak, would barely nod —
obeying, not agreeing. And the men,
who followed Lee as if he were a god,

in certain hope of triumph once again,
were sacrificed in thousands on the height.
Why rush to die? The dream was fading then:

our hopeless cause would soon devour the light.
Perhaps we should have waited for the night.

Flower Seller

Glimpsed roses at a roadside stall: so bright
a contrast to the city's traffic haze,
rich with the peace and warmth of summer's days
and quiet reveries of dark and light;
seen only for a moment — there, then gone.
Such wistful beauty, such a brave display,
stands out against the drabness of the day,
affirming even here that dreams live on.

But wayside seller, looking at your face,
I see your flowers are only goods to sell
with no innate significance. Ah well,
we see small value in the commonplace.
Still I wonder, trapped within life's schemes
and compromises, did you sell your dreams?

Who's Afraid?

My sister takes reception class and prides
herself on spinning yarns: at five years old
the kids when entertained are good as gold,
and learn a lot from fairy tales besides.
They loved the story of the pig who tries
to build a house of straw — the one the bold
and wicked wolf will wreck — a tale best told
in detail, showing all it signifies.

"The pig," she told them, "found a turnip bed
made out of straw and asked if he could dig
a little up. Guess what the farmer said?"
"I know," cried Jude, one hand above her head,
and standing (since she wasn't very big):
"Well, bugger me — here comes a talking pig!"

Bloodlines

They're pictured wearing baubles carved from bone,
woad-daubed and fur-clad, flaunting tribal scars.
Such disrespect — such crude depiction — mars
the memories embedded in the stone
and in my blood, my every chromosome.
Why paint their culture worthless next to ours,
those folk who traced the movement of the stars
and built Stonehenge before the birth of Rome?

Their mysteries live on within each cairn
and megalith, though little else remains:
like us they learned what pride and progress cost.
If we could call their spirits to return,
would they stand silent awed by all our gains —
or stricken, seeing everything we've lost?

On a Photograph of a Young Child

Shining eyes and golden hair,
little soldier standing there —
may the future take you where
stars will always shine at night,
days will all be golden-bright.
May the touch of care be light.

For My Daughter

It's funny how I never saw you grow.
I seem to miss what's nearest as a rule,
far too preoccupied — a busy fool
blind to the way the seasons come and go.

What shall I give since now you're going too
and will be gone a while? Although you're brave
and self-assured, I know I rarely gave
a sign to show how proud I was of you.

I give it now, with love; but love's no gift:
it's yours by right. Because you're going far
I'll give a gentle light to be your star,
and all my hopes to hold when life's adrift.

I'll give them all, though all I have would be
no gift beside the gift you were to me.

Harry Potter
(for TK)

For all the years, I still recall those rare
clairvoyant boyhood moments when my world
was new, and I glimpsed magic as it swirled
and scintillated in the morning air.

Grave young sorcerer, you make me smile
with broomsticks, spells and potions. Every charm
defies the Dark Lord, shields your friends from harm
and conjures up my childhood for a while.

Try to grow no older; take good care
to keep your youthful confidence and grace.
I will remember how your spirit shone
so bravely in the shadow of despair —
a talisman to ward us when we face
a world grown old with all its magic gone.

Cushioning the Blow

We thought it best to leave the cat with Ted
along with Grandma, when we went away.
No sooner were we home from holiday
than, bluntly, he announced the cat was dead.

"Listen!" I said. "Bad news is better told
obliquely — like this: 'Bess went climbing on
the roof and fell. Her legs and back were gone.
They tried to save her but she was too old.' "

Ted — who's direct but not a thoughtless man —
was chastened (so he said) and mortified.
"Don't worry, Cousin Edward," I replied,
"we all drop clangers. By the way, how's Gran?"

"Not great," he said. "In fact, to tell the truth,
last night she went out climbing on the roof…"

ABOUT THE AUTHOR

I was born in Ffestiniog, North Wales, brought up in Hull and educated at Hull Grammar School before going on to study modern history at St Catherine's College, Oxford.

I'm drawn to the creative tension between form and content so mostly write in rhyme and metre. There are various poetry forms in this book: sonnet, triolet, roundel, ballad, double dactyl, villanelle, hymnal stanza and limerick, along with some of my own creation and a few Japanese tanka.

I frequent various on-line poetry workshops and have received invaluable help and advice from them over the years. Special thanks to my friends at Eratosphere and Sonnet Central.

My life's been spent in the near aura of famous poets: Dafydd ap Gwilym, greatest of the Welsh bards; Philip Larkin, one-time librarian of Hull University; Andrew Marvell, a fellow-alumnus of Hull Grammar School. I now live with my wife in Stoke Poges, Buckinghamshire, a stone's throw from the churchyard where Thomas Gray is buried; still hoping that one day something of these poets will rub off on me.

You can contact me via my website:
www.davidgwilymanthony.co.uk

POETS' COMMENTS ON DAVID'S PREVIOUS BOOKS

Talking to Lord Newborough

If a poem is a verbal device designed to go off in the heart (apologies to Philip Larkin) then David G. Anthony's graceful, contemplative second collection implodes quietly, delivering emotional truths from within well-crafted constructs.

Cheryl Snell

David Anthony's superb new collection, *Talking to Lord Newborough,* is the second release by a remarkable new literary publisher, The Alsop Review Press... Anthony's poems are all written in traditional rhymed forms, but the poet's sensibility is entirely modern. Anthony is a master, so at home with such forms as the sonnet and the villanelle (to name only two) that the resulting poems are fluid and seamless, truly flawless. Equally notable is the broad range of tone and subject matter, from the wildly hilarious to the deeply moving. My personal favorites include "Situation Vacant" and the wistful title poem.

Robert L Smith

David Anthony is a skilled craftsman whose use of form always feels natural. Although he's at home with wordplay and metaphor, his work is not opaque. It often breaks the cardinal rules of contemporary poetry: Don't show any emotions other than anger and melancholy, don't use perfect rhymes, and for

God's sake, don't 'say' anything. That infuriates some critics — always a good sign.

R M Kelleher

There is no 'street cred' and no attempt to match or compete with the noise of modern media. This is poetry painstakingly composed in traditional forms that have changed very little and have stood the test of time…The subject matter is broad — from wistful to uncomfortable — from a commemoration of the late Queen Mother that concludes: 'Lie easy now, the head that wore a crown', to "Out of the Night", which examines our unforgiving attitude to a criminal who has taken the lives of many others. Some of the poems are funny and some of them are not. They are always honest and offer sympathy, but no quarter.

Peter Stewart Richards

Words to Say

David Anthony's work shows that a poem doesn't have to raise its voice to get our attention, and that control is not the opposite of feeling. These pages offer a rare enjoyment: contemporary verses that please the ear as well as the intellect.

Alicia E Stallings

A peopled landscape is always present. These poems will give great pleasure to those without expert knowledge and even more to those who realise how much skill was needed to produce such simplicity.

Janet Kenny

I was aware, while reading these poems, of his mastery of rhyme and metre, and overall, a voice of great dignity and control. There are many moving poems here, but also a section called 'Chestnut Puree' of some wickedly funny ones.

M A Griffiths

It's a wonderful book, truly. I've been picking it up and setting it down and picking it up again for the past two or three weeks. Every time I read it I find something I hadn't seen before. "For My Daughter" and "On the Suicide of a Friend" are my current favourites. I may have others tomorrow. The voice is gentle, soft-spoken and perceptive.

Jaimes Alsop

Words to Say is a wonderful book, full of all the right things that poetry ought to have: seriousness, moral weight, feeling, complexity, music, without any pretentiousness or self-consciousness or wrong notes. What the poet does with formal patterns is deft and casual, even a potentially hard one for English, like the Petrarchan sonnet. He manages to get real thought into the triolet, and he makes it feel natural. His rhymes, whether perfect or slant, seem inevitable. It's good to find among these poems several that are already familiar from some of the best sites on the internet; the unfamiliar ones are just as stunning and immediately inviting. The Foreword by Helena Nelson gets it right when it notes Anthony's 'delight in his craft'. This is beautiful work, enhanced by the art; I'm grateful to have it on this side of the Atlantic!

Rhina P Espaillat

The first things that came to my mind were the dignity and gravity of his work. His judgments are as measured as his verse.

Of course for the light of heart, he also writes a wicked versified joke.

Tim Murphy

David's poems are rarely mere ornaments: they contain real thought, often difficult thought at that. He is an honourable disciple in a long tradition, using the sonnet, for example, to introduce a question or problem, before offering his own considered resolution. His thought is compressed, personal and satisfying. Penetrating in his insights, he avoids didacticism. His utterance is characterised by interrogatives, perhapses, and a tone of conjecture. At the same time, he is playful with words, form and intent. Sometimes it is a very serious playfulness; at other times, it is unashamedly mischievous. The humorous poems in this collection are no less carefully made than their serious counterparts. They bubble up from an irrepressible sense of fun. Who could resist 'Cushioning the Blow' or 'Who's Afraid?' Such pieces serve to persuade that poetry can both begin and end in delight… Faced with sadnesses both small and large, David Anthony's poems, with disarming modesty and memorable grace, really do find "the proper words to say". Read them, and you will see.

Helena Nelson

AND ON HIS POEMS

The scene and situation are set at once, so that communication is clear at the surface level. The mystery occurs at a deeper level, and is subtler, in what the poem suggests about memory and time: "These days the past is nearer". We think of the past as retreating into a farther distance, as do the dead, but this poem reverses that notion, and implies that the dead "remember" with us. I found myself feeling not only surprised, but persuaded by this tender but unsentimental sense of identification with those who are closer than they were when they "left" us, because now we're approaching them. The end feels wholly true, and the force of the poem is greater than it would have been if the language were not so unobtrusively ordinary. And then, just to compound the strangeness of the poem, a re-reading reminds you that this particular "old friend" was a stranger, after all, "met" beside his gravestone by an imaginative and sensitive boy! Remarkable poem.

Rhina P Espaillat (Judge, Eratosphere poetry competition 2004) on the poem "Talking to Lord Newborough"

This is not just a poem to please its author, or the denizens of a workshop. It is cunningly, perniciously calculated to snare the judge of a poetry competition. I undertook this charge resolutely determined to exclude any poem about poetry from the finalists. 'Slush Pile' has defeated my good intentions. I will never forgive the author, when I learn his or her identity.

Alan Sullivan (Judge, Eratosphere sonnet competition 2007) on the poem "Slush Pile"

David's poem illustrates that there is yet life in traditional forms and themes when handled with skill. The 'hymn stanza' (alternating lines of iambic tetrameter and iambic trimeter) and the repetitions serve to reinforce the tone of the piece rather than distracting from it and clearly demonstrate the truth of Prokoffief's observation, when he was asked why he alone of 20th Century composers continued to write in traditional key signatures: 'There are so many lovely things yet to be said in C Major.'

Howard Miller on the poem "Warming"

Getting lost in the woods is a narrative which belongs to folklore, childhood and the pre-industrial human past: it is one to which the atavistic instincts of the modern urban reader still strongly respond. This poem plays effectively with process (narrative but also formal). Within the miniature span of the poem, we nevertheless have a sense of time passing and dangerous night approaching. Judiciously placed punctuation varies the traction of two important little words — 'now' and 'because'. The two foreshortened lines reflect the ebb and flow of the speaker's confidence. Line six offers a burst of cheery optimism — 'I'll find the track somehow.' — but the conclusion again casts doubt on a happy outcome, and the poem records a mood of uncertainty and a shadowy sense of threat. The title implies, perhaps, that the path will be found. Let's hope it doesn't lead to Baba Yaga's hut… "Passing through the Woods" is exemplary.

Carol Rumens (The Guardian) on the title poem

INDEX OF POEMS

A La Cart	24
A Winter Funeral	12
Bird's Eye View	40
Bloodlines	61
Crossing the Border	44
Cushioning the Blow	65
English Weathercock	30
Father of the Man	5
Flotsam on a Winter's Tide	4
Flower Seller	59
For All the Saints	42
For My Daughter	63
Four Views of Kyoto	53
Gatekeepers	9
Harry Potter	64
Hawthorn	27
Heilige Nacht	55
I Thought You Were a Friend	14
In a Storm	8
Knowing the Score	43
Late August at Hadrian's Wall	29
Look Away	57
Mother's Day	22
My Bulkhead Light	36
Navigator	10
Nearer to Thee	18
Older the Worse	31
On a Photograph of a Young Child	62

On first looking into Chapman's Homer	39
On the Death of the Queen Mother	21
On the Suicide of a Friend	23
One-Way Ticket	50
Out of the Night	17
Over America	56
Passing through the Woods	2
Pickett's Charge	58
Plague	45
Remembered Wings	15
Saint Patrick's Day Parade, Yokohama	52
Situation Vacant	51
Slush Pile	37
Stuffing it In	35
Summer's End	3
Talking to Lord Newborough	47
Tallyman	28
Tambourine Man	54
The Road Taken	6
To Die For	20
To Gerard Manley Hopkins	48
To My Muse	38
Triolet	34
Unsaid	13
Walking the Dog	7
Warming	32
Water Bearer	46
Wede Away	26
Who'll Hold Their Hands?	16
Who's Afraid?	60
Words to Say	19